OF WALDEN POND

Henry David Thoreau,
Frederic Tudor,
—and—
the Pond Between

LESA CLINE-RANSOME

Illustrated by
ASHLEY BENHAM-YAZDANI

HOLIDAY HOUSE • NEW YORK

2

WINTER

Henry David Thoreau
fled
the city of Concord
for the woods
leaving behind
family
church
and work
for the company
of sparrows and squirrels
chickadees and woodchucks
a journal
his pencil
and the poetry
of Walden Pond

Frederic Tudor
failed at
one venture
after another
a laughingstock
to his neighbors
he left behind
family
Boston
debts
and headed
for the woods
with tools and 100 men
sleds and horses
a journal
his pencil
and the riches
of Walden Pond

Oddball
tax dodger
nature lover
dreamer

That's what they called
Thoreau

Bankrupt
disgrace
good for nothing
dreamer

That's what they called
Tudor

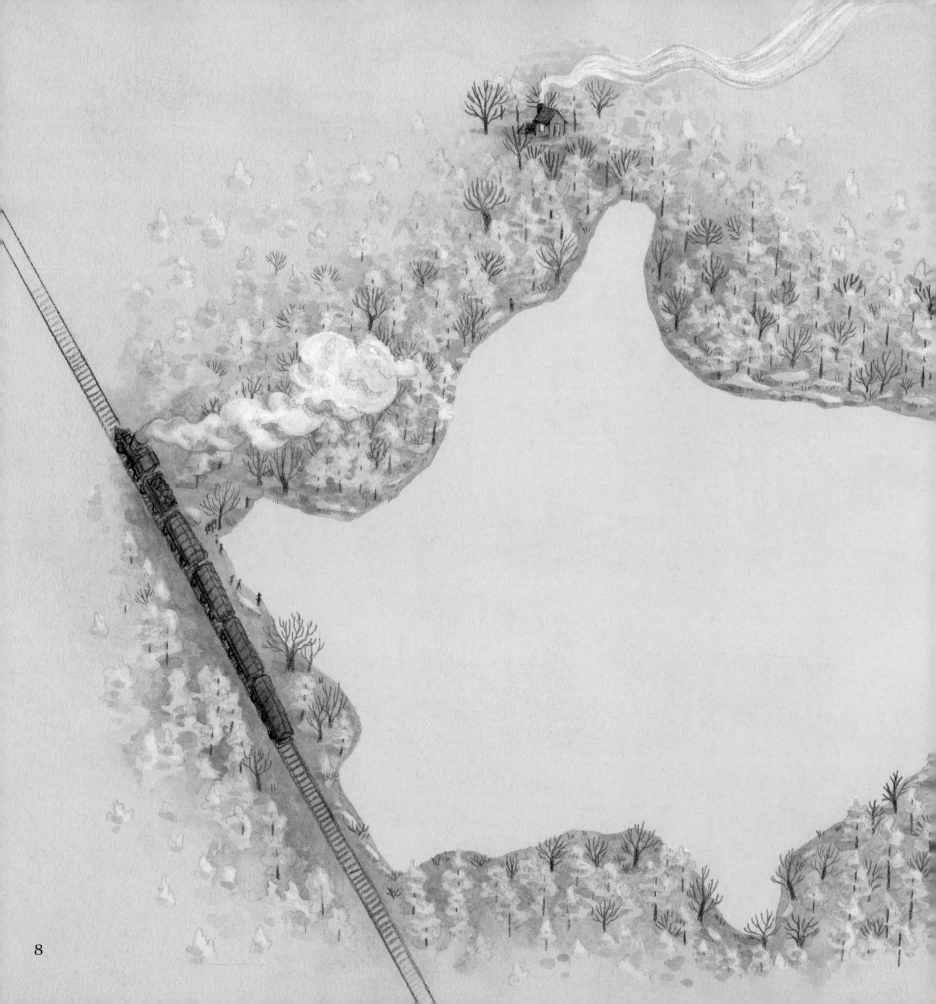

A pond in the woods
of Concord
circled by pine and oak
home to perch and pickerel
dressed in a coat of
winter white
an inspiration for Thoreau
a harvest for Tudor
a bounty for both
sat the frozen waters
of Walden Pond

Tudor and his men
arrived
at first light
at the water's edge
and unloaded
awls and cleavers
chisels and clippers
from horses and sleds

Tudor ordered
work to begin
a harvest
from the ice
of Walden Pond

While Tudor unloaded
Thoreau watched
from the window
of his tiny cabin
built with his hands
to hold
one bed
one table
three chairs
a desk
just room enough
to write
of the wonders
of nature
and of waters
"lying between the earth and the heavens"
of Walden Pond

While Thoreau watched
horses clopped
onto the ice
on metal spiked shoes
dragging sharp blades behind
first forward
then across
cutting lines
into ice
perfect squares
of Walden Pond

While horses clopped
Thoreau pulled on boots
and walked down
to the pond
to study
the men who
"Unroof the house of fishes"
whose drilling
sawing and hammering
 of ice
silenced the song
of the
chickadee
nuthatch
and woodpecker
and shattered
the frozen stillness
of Walden Pond

While Thoreau pulled on boots
Tudor reviewed
his "Ice Diary"
one hundred eighty tons of ice
one full acre of harvest
sixteen days of work
three months of storage
"Let those laugh who win"
the first
the only
to voyage
across the equator
with the ice
of Walden Pond

While Tudor reviewed
Thoreau wrote
"Thus it appears
that the sweltering inhabitants...
Of Madras and Bombay
And Calcutta,
drink at my well"

SPRING

Days grew long
warmer
brighter
Honeysuckle breezes
thawed ice into
rippling waters
reflecting the majesty of
pine
oak
and maple trees
from the waters
of Walden Pond

Blocks of ice
blanketed in sawdust
and hay
stacked
as high as the hills
grew shorter
every day
waiting
on the shores
of Walden Pond

SUMMER

While Thoreau wrote
the ship *Delhi*
set sail
loaded by Tudor's men
with blocks
of ice
sealed in
wood
packed in
tanbark
hay
straw
stowed below deck
out of the summer sun
for the long voyage south
across the Atlantic
far from the waters
of Walden Pond

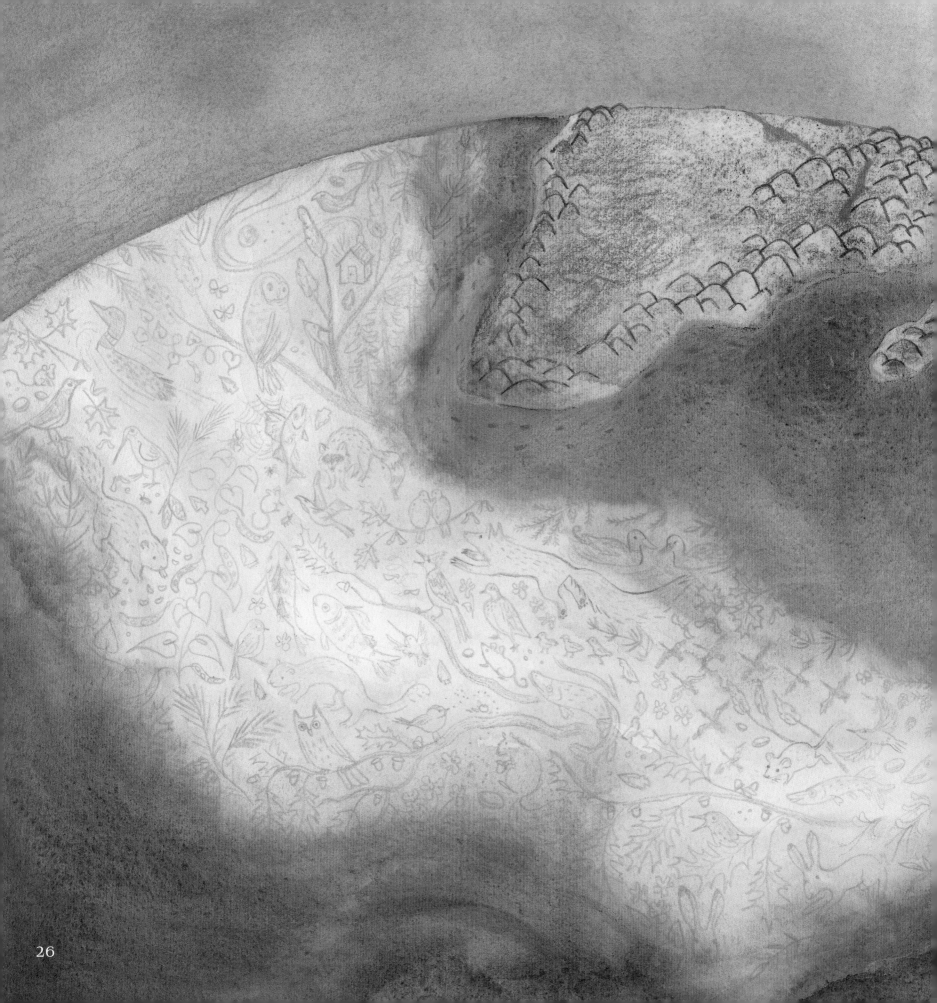

While the *Delhi*
sailed for Calcutta
drip by drip
pound by pound
day by day
month by month
ice
profits
hope
melted a trail of Walden Pond
from Boston
across the Atlantic
to Calcutta

FALL

While the *Delhi*
docked in Calcutta
Thoreau wrote
of fall New England breezes
the loon
the owl
the woods
and of ice
"The pure Walden water
is mingled with
The sacred water
of the Ganges"
From pond to river
Concord to Calcutta
running waters
frozen into sweet
solid cubes
of Walden Pond

29

While the docks
of Calcutta
flooded with
melting ice
workers carried blocks
on their backs
to Tudor ice houses
while crowds gathered
whispering
gasping
pointing
daring to touch
the glistening objects
burning them
with the cold
of Walden Pond

31

Miles from Concord
the wealthy
of Calcutta
cooled
with chilled delights
ice cream and
frozen cubes in crystal glasses
clinking in celebration
To Tudor!
To ice!
To Walden Pond!

a philosopher
a naturalist
a poet

That's what they called
Thoreau

an inventor
a genius
an ice king

That's what they called
Tudor

WINTER

A pond in the woods
of Concord
an inspiration for Thoreau
a harvest for Tudor
a bounty for both
Circled by pine and oak
home to perch and pickerel
dressed in a coat of
winter white
sit
the frozen waters
of Walden Pond

AUTHOR'S NOTE

Henry David Thoreau was an essayist and poet who wrote his most famous work, *Walden or, Life in the Woods*, while living for two years, two months, and two days in the woods of Concord, Massachusetts, from 1845 to 1847. From his cabin, on land borrowed from his friend and fellow writer Ralph Waldo Emerson, 28-year-old Thoreau watched Frederic Tudor harvest ice from his window and recorded it in his journal. His commitment to civil disobedience in the name of a greater good once led to an arrest for refusing to pay his poll tax. As a transcendentalist, familiar with Indian texts, Thoreau was fascinated by the idea that ice from the Walden Pond he so loved would be shipped to and enjoyed in India.

Frederic Tudor was a struggling Boston entrepreneur when he dreamed up the idea of shipping ice harvested from New England to tropical climates. His first attempts to sell ice in Havana, Cuba; Charleston, South Carolina; and the Caribbean were such financial failures that he was jailed for failure to repay his debts and ridiculed by Boston townspeople for what most considered a preposterous idea.

A reporter for a February 19, 1806 article in the *Boston Gazette* wrote, "No joke. A vessel with a cargo of 80 tones of Ice has cleared out from this port for Martinique. We hope this will not prove a slippery speculation." Tudor, however, remained convinced that selling ice to India could turn his fortune around. His inventive methods of storing the ice ensured that much of his harvest remained intact until it was ready to set sail on its maiden 14,000-mile voyage on May 12, 1834. Of the one hundred and eighty tons that left the Boston harbor, approximately one hundred ten arrived in Calcutta on September 10. Sales were brisk, and for the first time ever, Tudor made a profit of nearly $2,000.

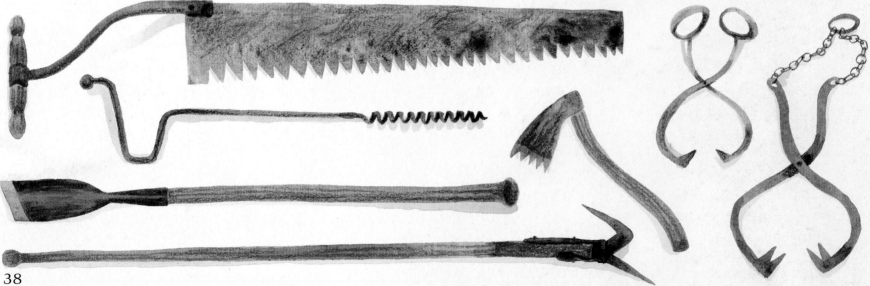

Over the next decade, as the ice trade gained momentum, sources to harvest ice became increasingly scarce, and in the winter of 1846-47, Tudor bought the rights to begin harvesting on Walden Pond. It was there that the worlds of Tudor and Thoreau intersected.

Both men were drawn to Walden Pond for vastly different reasons. Thoreau's retreat to the woods allowed him to write in solitude, live simply, and commune with nature, while Tudor thrived on attaining wealth and regaining his status in society.

Henry David Thoreau's works have influenced Robert Frost, Martin Luther King Jr., and Mohandas Gandhi. In addition to writing on his experiences as a naturalist and conservationist, his essay *Civil Disobedience* offered a groundbreaking historic and compelling argument against the institution of slavery. Thoreau died in 1862 at 45 years old. His final word was "moose."

Tudor's ice business grew into a huge success and he revolutionized the ice industry until his death in 1864 at the age of 80 years old. His innovations in shipping and insulation were used in the commercial ice harvesting industry for residential ice boxes in the United States, our early versions of refrigerators. Tudor became known as "The Ice King."

When Tudor sent ice to India, he was shipping it to the infamous East India Company, a British corporation which had become the de facto ruler of much of India. In the early 17th century, the Company began to get a foothold in India, which at that time was part of the Mughal Empire. Throughout the 17th and 18th centuries, the Company competed with other European trading companies also exploiting the vast natural resources of India and other less affluent countries, which left India's inhabitants impoverished and living in famine. The Company became so powerful that by 1833, when Tudor began shipping ice to India, it ruled vast parts of India, including Calcutta (now called Kolkata). It is most likely that it was the British from the East India Company, and not the Indians of Calcutta, who enjoyed Tudor's shipments of ice.

For Mike Kristofik, who eased my fears with stories and endless inspiration —L. C.-R

For Dara, with love and gratitude even deeper than the sparkling waters of Walden Pond —A.B.-Y

The author would like to thank Rekha Nori for reading the manuscript and reviewing the art. Also: The words in quotes on pages 12, 16, 18, 20, and 28 are taken directly from Thoreau's diary.

Text copyright © 2022 by Lesa Cline-Ransome • Illustrations copyright © 2022 by Ashley Benham-Yazdani

HOLIDAY HOUSE is registered in the U.S. Patent and Trademark Office. • Printed and bound in September 2022 at Phoenix Color, Hagerstown, MD, USA. • www.holidayhouse.com

3 5 7 9 10 8 6 4 2

First Edition

Library of Congress Cataloging-in-Publication Data

Names: Cline-Ransome, Lesa, author. | Benham-Yazdani, Ashley, illustrator. • Title: Of Walden Pond / by Lesa Cline-Ransome ; illustrated by Ashley Benham-Yazdani.

Description: First edition. | New York : Holiday House, [2022] | Audience: Ages 4–8 | Audience: Grades K–1 | Summary: "The story of Henry David Thoreau's time at Walden Pond is contrasted with businessman Frederic Tudor's scheme to cut 180 tons of ice from Walden Pond and transport it to India"— Provided by publisher.

Identifiers: LCCN 2021036072 | ISBN 9780823448586 (hardcover) | Subjects: LCSH: Walden Pond (Middlesex County, Mass.)—Juvenile literature. | Ice industry—Juvenile literature. | Nature—Juvenile literature.

Thoreau, Henry David, 1817–1862—Juvenile literature. | Tudor, Frederic, 1783–1864—Juvenile literature.

Classification: LCC F72.M7 C6 2022 | DDC 974.4/4—dc23 • LC record available at https://lccn.loc.gov/2021036072

ISBN: 978-0-8234-4858-6 (hardcover)

All Rights Reserved